KUTTANAD SOILS:

MANAGEMENT APPROACHES FOR RICE PRODUCTION

KUTTANAD SOILS: MANAGEMENT APPROACHES FOR RICE PRODUCTION

Authors

Rohith A K

Dr. Biju Joseph

Dr. Kota Adilakshmi

Rahul Chandra

Namitha Krishna

Edition I
2025

Self-Publishing

Published in consortium with Notion Press

Citation:

Rohith, A. K., Joseph, B., Adilakshmi, K., Rahul, C., and Namitha, K. 2025. *Kuttanad Soils: Management Approaches for Rice Production* (1st ed., Vol. 1). 56p. [Online].

Contact

Ph: +91 9495718198
+91 9074664572

Mail: rohith-2020-11-030@student.kau.in

FORWARD

The Kuttanad region of Kerala, often referred to as the "Rice Bowl of Kerala," holds a unique agricultural heritage. However, the acid sulfate soils of this region pose significant challenges to sustainable crop production. Characterized by severe acidity due to the presence of jarosites, iron, aluminum, and manganese, alongside salinity concerns from seawater intrusion, these soils demand extensive management strategies. Furthermore, while rich in organic matter, their nutrient availability is limited, making rice cultivation particularly challenging.

This book, *KUTTANAD SOILS: MANAGEMENT APPROACHES FOR RICE PRODUCTION,* delves into the intricate properties of these problem soils and explores innovative approaches for their management. Traditional practices like liming are revisited alongside modern techniques such as the use of organic amendments, including rice husk ash, biochar, and green manures, to neutralize acidity and improve soil fertility. The book also highlights the potential of genetic tolerance in rice varieties, phyto-mining techniques, and critical land amendments to ensure sustainable rice production in this region.

By synthesizing existing knowledge and presenting practical solutions, this book serves as a comprehensive guide for researchers, agronomists, and farmers. It is an effort to bridge the gap between science and practice, supporting both agricultural productivity and environmental conservation. We hope this work inspires further research and innovation in addressing the challenges of acid sulfate soils, ensuring the prosperity of Kuttanad's agricultural landscape.

Rohith A K
Biju Joseph
Kota Adilakshmi
Rahul Chandra
Namitha Krishna

PREFACE

The **Kuttanad region** in Kerala, known for its rice cultivation, faces unique challenges due to its **acid sulphate soils**. These soils are highly acidic due to the presence of jarosites, iron (Fe), aluminum (Al), and manganese (Mn), and are further complicated by **salinity** from coastal proximity. Although rich in organic matter, the nutrient imbalance in these soils makes rice cultivation difficult.

This book, **"Kuttanad Soils: Management Approaches for Rice Production,"** explores various soil management strategies to address these challenges. It discusses traditional methods such as **liming**, alongside innovative approaches including the use of **organic amendments** (rice husk ash, biochar, green manures), **genetically tolerant rice varieties**, and **phyto-mining** techniques and various other management approached to improve soil health and fertility.

This book serves as a valuable resource for understanding the intricate dynamics of Kuttanad soils, offering farmers, researchers, agronomist and policymakers, practical solutions to manage acid sulfate soils effectively. Furthermore, it lays the foundation for future research, encouraging the continued exploration of new management techniques and their potential to support sustainable rice production in this challenging yet important agricultural region.

Dr. Rani. B.
Professor and Head
Department of Soil Science and Agricultural Chemistry
College of Agriculture, Vellayani

CONTENTS

INTRODUCTION

Kerala is well-known for its astonishing backwaters, ecotourism initiatives, mesmerizing beauty, enthralling beaches, and delicious cuisine, but it is well gripped with agriculture. The state is looking forward with innovations and developments in crop production, especially in rice. Globally recognized agricultural heritage system called Kuttanad, is a low-lying deltaic region which is occupied in below and Mean Sea Level (MSL). Kuttanad is the major region where rice is cultivated extensively and hence this region is known as the "rice bowl of Kerala". So, it is obligatory that such a region should be prepared for producing rice. The key crop of Kuttanad is paddy, and it is farmed mainly in puncha season (November - March). 20% of the total rice production of Kerala state is reported from Kuttanad. The region is warm and humid, with moderate seasonal temperature variation (21-38°C) and 300 cm of average annual rainfall, 83 percent of which falls during two monsoon seasons from June to October. More than the ingenuity of management systems of farming under below sea level, the agricultural and biological diversity and a hoard of indigenous knowledge make Kuttanad farming system distinctive (Padmakumar, 2013). The production of paddy from this region is drastically declining over a period of time. Many farmers even left farming. This region comes under problematic soils due to its acidic condition. To evolve a suitable acidity amelioration/management technology, the characterization of soil acidity is most warranted. Studies on characteristics of acid sulphate soils were done by many workers (Indira and Covilakam, 2013) Specific practices for crop production and soil and nutrient management systems were developed for rice. Many of them are widely accepted and economical. These systems of crop production are inevitable to keep the productivity in consistency and to improve the yield and give out maximum profits.

CHAPTER - 1

THE KUTTANAD SOIL

Kuttanad is a low-lying area (0.6-2.2 m below Mean Sea Level (MSL)) with soils of highly acidic nature containing high level of toxic salts. Of the 50,000 ha of rice fields of kuttanad, around 15000 ha belongs to acid sulphate soils (Typic Sulfaquent) which constitutes mostly the kari lands, the most problematic cultivated area (Indira and Covilakam, 2013). This land is drawn-out over a geographic area of 854 km^2 in three southern districts of Kerala state viz., Kottayam, Pathanamthitta and Alappuzha. It is the largest wetland habitat in India (760 19' to 760 33' E; 90 17' to 90 40' N). The Vembanadu Lake, the largest Ramsar site in India, is surrounded by a huge delta formed by five rivers, including Achenkovil, Pampa, Manimala, Meenachil, and Moovattupuzha, which flow down from the Western Ghats. These poorly drained potential acid sulphate soils contain high level of pyrites (Neenu *et al.,* 2020). Based on soil morphology, soils of Kuttanad are classified into Kayal lands (13000 ha.), Karappadams (33000 ha.) and Kari lands (9000 ha.) (Chattopadhyay and Sidharthan, 1985; Aparna *et al.,* 2020).

i. Kayal lands - reclaimed beds from Vembanad Lake and are located in Kuttanad and Kottayam taluks.
ii. Karappadams - situated along the waterways and lakes, mainly in the eastern and southern parts of Kottayam district
iii. Kari lands – They are swampy area with black peaty soil seen in northern (Thuravoor and vaikom-vadayar areas) and in southern (purakkad) extremities of kuttanad.

Acid sulphate soils of kuttanad are belong to 6 series soil series such as

1. Ambalapuzha,
2. Thuravoor,
3. Vaikom,
4. Kallara,
5. Purakkad,
6. Thakazhi.

These soils are classified under the order Entisols, suborder Aquents, great group Sulfaquents and sub group Typic Sulfaquents (Beena, 2005). Kari soils of Kuttanad are with lower pH, due to the acid sulphate nature of the soil and the presence of undecomposed organic matter. The organic matter in these soils is predominantly ligno-protein complex comprising large quantities of lignin, ether and alcohol soluble substances and some cellulose and polyceronoides. Kari soils and the wood fossils associated with them are found to contain different forms of sulphur such as free, organically combined sulfide and sulphate forms (Neenu *et al.,* 2020).

Acid sulphate soils contain metal sulfides. Undisturbed and waterlogged state of these soils may not cause any risk. However, when these soils are exposed to oxygen, chemical oxidation process will take place and they produces sulphuric acid which brings these soils to so called acid sulphate soils. The strongly acidic condition, directly affects the growth and development of crops with a result of aluminum and iron toxicity and it also causes declining of the phosphorus availability and other nutrients. Fe and Al toxicity are very wide spread in acid sulphate areas of Kuttanad often leading to a decline of yield of 50 - 70 % (Thampatti *et al.,* 2005). Thereby Kuttanad showed a loss of soil health and fall in cropped area. Another major problem is the low inflow into Kuttanad during summer months (Feb-May) which leads to an increase in salinity, acidity and lack of water. (Aparna *et al.,* 2020).

CHAPTER - 2

GENESIS OF ACID SULPHATE SOIL

Acid sulphate soils are formed from parent material other than marine and estuarine sediments (Chenery, 1954; Poelman, 1973). The environmental conditions under which acid sulphate soils are formed include a tropical climate, flat topography and vegetation (Thorton and Giglioli, 1965)

Genesis of acid sulphate soil includes three main stages, the cumulative and reductive geochemical phase, oxidative phase and neutralization phase. Geochemical phase includes the sedimentary pyrite formation which involves bacterial reduction of sulphate to sulphide, partial oxidation of sulphide to elemental Sulphur and interaction between ferrous or ferric ion with sulphide and elemental Sulphur (Ponnamperuma, 1984).

The main chemical reactions are as follows

$$SO_4^{2-} + 4H_2 + 2H^+ \longrightarrow H_2S + 4H_2O$$

$$H_2S + O_2 \longrightarrow S + H_2O$$

$$Fe^{2+} + S^{2-} \longrightarrow FeS$$

$$FeS + S \longrightarrow FeS_2$$

In the oxidative phase, pyrite will get oxidized with lowering of water table and the overall reaction can be expressed as

$$FeS_2 + 7/2\ O_2 + H_2O \longrightarrow Fe^{2+} + 2SO4^{2-} + 2H^+$$

Bacteria like *Thiobacillus ferroidans* could enhance the rate of reaction of this reaction (Van Breemen, 1973; Bloomfield and coulter, 1973). Neutralization phase experience the reaction of sulphuric acid with bases in the sediments. Extensive acidification occurs if the amount of sulphates in soil is higher compared to the soil sediments.

Rice Field View from RRS Moncompu - captured by Rohith. *et al.* (2024)

CHAPTER - 3

SOIL PROPERTIES

The physical, chemical, and biological properties of the soil affect the soil structure by providing means to unify soil aggregates. Short-term degradation of soil structure can cause a decrease in water filtration and an increase in erosion (Juhrian *et al.,* 2020). Organic matter plays an important role in aggregation and no organic matter contributes to unstable soil structre (Gomez, 2016). Clay minerals influence the physical and chemical soil properties such as swelling ability. Mechanical soil resistance reflects the resistance in the soil against penetration and is related to soil compaction, and is related to soil bulk density (Juhrian *et al.,* 2020).

Physical Properties

Kuttanad soils are dark brown to black in colour which represents the richness in organic matter content in soil. The soils are sticky and plastic, sub angular blocky structure and sandy to clayey in nature with random deposits of lime shells and humus (Thampatti, 1997). Kuttanad clay have a natural moisture content of 90% and an optimum moisture content of 33% with specific gravity 2.02 Mg m^{-3} and maximum dry density 1.36 Mg m^{-3} (Bindhu and Ramabhadran, 2011). Bulk density mean values obtained from Kuttanad soil, ranged between 0.79-0.99 Mg.m^{-3}. The pore water salinity of Kuttanad soil was found to be 4.49 g/l. The pore water salinity appears to be reasonably high and it is capable of increasing the inter-particle forces (Suganya, and Sivapullaiah, 2015).

As stated by Thampatti and Jose (2000), in Kuttanad soils the physical properties like water holding capacity, pore space and hydraulic conductivity increase with depth evidently on account of increased clay and organic carbon content. In Typic Sulfaquents even though the clay content was very high, due to the large quantity of organic matter, horizon recorded very high value for hydraulic conductivity. The bulk density was also lowest for this layer. The peculiar position of Kuttanad also restricted the profile development in the tract. The soil physical properties were not affected by the soil environmental change from a predominantly saline environment to a fresh water condition. The fluvial deposition during monsoons and impact of tidal intrusion even for the short period might have retarded the changes in physical characteristics.

Chemical Properties

The chemical properties of Typic Sulfaquents did not show a definite patttern of variation. In kuttand soils saline water intrusion is a major problem and was able to remove much of exchangeable acidity from the soils. Van Mensvoort *et al.,* (1981) pointed out that in acid sulphate soils $A1^{3+}$ can be substituted by Na^{+} and Mg^{2+} in salt or brackish water which will help to lower the exchangeable acidity of the soil (Thampatti and Jose, 2000). The acid release from the sulfuric horizon is attributed to the reason for the extreme acidity of these soils. On comparing the existing acidity parameters with that reported during the pre-barrage period (Money 1961; Kabeerathumma 1969, 1975; Nair and Subramoney 1969; Money and Sukumaran 1973). Indira and Covilakom (2013) have reported a pH range of 2.5 to 5.2 in Kuttanad soils.

In case of EC, the tidal and fluvial effect varied with the climate in each year and this resulted in variation in chemical characteristics. Considerable reduction in electrical conductivity was noted in the area during the post-barrage period when compared to that of pre-barrage period (Thampatti and Jose, 2000). The prevention of saline water intrusion from the sea, was the major source of salts, had decreased electrical conductivity of these soils. Extremely saline soils have changed to mildly saline soils. Nair and Pillai (1990) reported 90 per cent reduction in salinity during the months of March to May compared to that of pre-barrage period. Kuttanad soils have CEC: 8.60 cmol(+)Kg^{-1} and AEC:3.49 cmol(-)Kg^{-1}- Arya Lekshmi (2016)

Table 1: pH and EC of surface and sub surface soils of Kari series

Soil samples	Ambalapuzha-subsurface	Ambalapuzha-surface	Purakkad-subsurface	Purakkad-surface	Thakazhi-subsurface	Thakazhi-surface	Kallara-subsurface	Kallara- surface	Thuravoor-subsurface	Thuravoor-surface	Vaikom-subsurface	Vaikom- surface
pH	4.0	4.4	4.0	4.0	4.8	4.6	4.1	4.1	2.9	2.4	4.0	4.0
EC (ds/m)	0.20	0.73	1.15	1.71	0.20	0.26	0.73	1.26	7.59	8.75	0.15	0.16

According to Aparna *et al.* (2020), the pH of Kuttanad soils ranges from 2.4 to 4.8. Thuravoor series showed lower surface pH value and higher EC values while Thakazhi series showed high pH value and Vaikom series shoes lowest EC value. (Table 1) The subsurface soil acidity might be also one of the reasons for the extreme acidity in Kuttanad soils.

Table 2: Organic Matter and Organic Carbon Content of the Kari Soil (%)

Soil samples	Ambalapuzha-subsurface	Ambalapuzha-surface	Purakkad-subsurface	Purakkad-surface	Thakazhi-subsurface	Thakazhi-surface	Kallara-subsurface	Kallara-surface	Thuravoor-subsurface	Thuravoor-surface	Vaikom-subsurface	Vaikom-surface
O.C	1.17	1.93	1.01	1.28	1.92	1.94	2.96	3.01	2.41	2.80	1.69	2.00
O.M	2.01	3.33	1.74	2.20	3.31	3.35	5.10	5.18	4.15	4.82	2.91	3.45

Aparna *et al,* (2020) reported that kuttanad soils are rich with organic matter and organic carbon contents. (Table 2) Kallara series shows the highest OM value and Purakkad series shows lowest values. Waterlogging associated with rice cropping might have enhanced the accumulation of organic carbon. The presence of sand layers, differential accumulation of organic matter and sedimentary nature of the parent materials are attributed to be the reason for the heterogeneity in organic carbon distribution. During the post-barrage period a severe depletion in soil organic matter was noted. The highest organic matter of 5.14 % reported in Kallara soils might be also due to enrichment of weed biomass and paddy straw in the cultivated fallows (Pillai and Subrahmanyan, 1929; Fores and Comin, 1987). Beena (2005) also observed highest organic carbon content of 5.35 % in Kallara soils.

Table:3 Mineral Content of Soil

Mineral	Percentage
Kaolinite	34.3%
Smectite	18.32%
Illite	6-12%
Chlorite	0-11%
Vermiculite	0-5%
Amphibole	0-4%
Gibbsite	0-17%
Quartz	0-2%
Feldspar	0-2%

The above table portrays the percentage of contents of various minerals present in the acid sulphate soils of Kuttanad region and it is clear that Kaolinite mineral is supreme and followed by Smectite and Illite.

Biological Properties

Mineralization of soil organic nitrogen, decomposition of rice straw and compost applied in soil etc. are various metabolic reactions in soils, which are carried out with soil micro-organisms, thereby these reactions supporting rice production as well as maintaining the fertility of paddy soils of Kuttanad (Kikuchi *et al.,* 2007). Biogeochemical cycles, plant production, microbial transformations, nutrient availability, pollutant removal, heavy metal chemistry, atmospheric exchange and sediment transport are the wetland functions determined by the biogeochemistry of wetland paddy soils

(Schoner *et al.,* 2009*).* A study was concluded by Smily *et al,* (2012) to determine the changes in soil microflora of paddy fields in relation to the type of farming system. A total of 11 bacterial species were isolated from paddy field soil whereas 15 were obtained from fish-rice rotational farming soil. The highest frequency of occurrence among paddy field isolates was the *Bacillus* spp. followed by *Klebsiella pneumoniae, K. oxytoca and Pseudomonas* spp.

In acid sulphate soils like kuttanad the existence of a bacterial sulphur cycle is proved by the presence of 'Sulphur oxidising' and sulphur reducing bacteria, where organic form of sulphur is converted to sulphuric acid form through the inorganic sulphides and sulphates. The presence of labile organic carbon and dissolved sulphate under anaerobic conditions provide an ideal environment for sulphate reducing bacteria. The production of sulphuric acid by this way is responsible for the low pH in Kari soils (Neenu *et al.,* 2020).

Paddy fields are observed with large organic carbon contents, meanwhile coconut fields are reporting as better carbon sink and emits only diminished quantity of methane (Chacko *et al.,* 2014). Labile carbons indicating the change of soil organic carbon and soil quality, acts as an active carbon pool, in which soil microbial activities contributes for soil carbon quantity (Jinbo *et al.,* 2006; Yang *et al.,* 2009). In rice soils 2-4% of total carbon pool belongs to the soil microbial biomass, and it represents the most labile soil organic matter and this pool turned over very rapidly (Reichardt *et al.,* 1997). Soil organic matter decomposition and nutrient recycling are regulated by soil microbial biomass carbon. Hence it could play essential role in maintain the sustainability and function of terrestrial ecosystem (Dhanya, 2017).

Soil organic matter content affects the enzyme activity (Dalal, 1975). Enzyme activity is contributed by the accumulated enzymes and also by enzymes produced from proliferating microorganisms (Kiss *et al.,* 1975). Various enzyme activities viz urease, amidase, phosphatase, arylsulphatase and glucoside activities were inhibited by water logging (Pulford and Tabatabai, 1988)

Carbon proportion was found to be highest in kallara series and rice land use system, while lowest in thottapalli series and rice fish use system. It is clear that soil series and land use system influenced the carbon turnover rate with the maximum value of 1.15 in thottapalli series and coconut land use, while minimum is at kallara and rice land use.

Table 4: Carbon proportion and turnover in acid sulphate soils

Soil series/Land use	Carbon proportion (POC/SOC)	Carbon turn over (MC/SOC)
Soil series		
S_1 – Ambalapuzha	0.35	0.82
S_2 – Purakkad	0.40	0.85
S_3 – Thakazhi	0.38	0.63
S_4 – Thuravur	0.29	0.64
S_5 – Thottapalli	0.25	1.15
S_6 – Kallara	0.62	0.27
Land use		
L_1 – Rice	0.54	0.54
L_2 – Coconut	0.39	0.70
L_3 - Rice – fish	0.36	0.60

CHAPTER - 4

FLOOD IMPACTS ON KUTTANAD SOIL

Kerala witnessed two consecutive floods in 2018 and 2019. The flood of 2018 is considered as the severest among them, which caused series of changes in physical, chemical and biological processes that influence soil quality. The nature, pattern and magnitude of these changes in soil properties due to submergence, depend on soil and submergence period (Ponnamperuma, 1984).

Arya (2020) studied the impact of 2018 flood on soils of AEU 4 of Kuttanad. The results revealed that, after the flood Kuttanad soils exhibited copious changes in its characters. The mean values for EC of affected soils varied from 0.36 to 0.88 dS m^{-1} and 98.67 % of soils reported an EC value under 1 dS m^{-1}. While the pH of the soil is in extreme acidity, that ranges from 3.54 to 4.79 due to the presence of iron sulphide oxidation. Also, the bulk density of most of the soil sample remained less than the optimum value of 1.33 Mg m^{-3}. Similarly particle density of most of the soil samples remained below 2.2 Mg m^{-3}. As a textural variation, Sandy clay loam appeared in 41.34% of total area followed by clay loam and sandy loam. Clay and silt particles of the soil give larger surface area, which allows more water holding capacity of the soils, in a range of 32-58.5%. Meanwhile organic carbon level of soils observed as greater than 1.5% and under flooded condition the organic matter decomposition was slower but it came in the range of 2.67- 3.00%, meanwhile variations of N, P and K are in 188-602 kg/ha, 5.79-

24.2 kg/ha and 252- 672 kg/ha respectively. After flood, higher deposition of Ca and Mg is recorded due to sediment deposition through the saline water intrusion coupled with the effect of liming material amendment in soil (Arya, 2020). Both Ca and Mg was in adequate rate of >300 mg/Kg and 226 - 634 mg/kg respectively. Arya (2020) concluded that on comparing with pre-flood, there is no significant increase in sulphur content after flood (94.5% soils were sufficient in sulphur content). Soils with jarosite minerals reported highest value for available sulphate. Water soluble S was negatively correlated with pH and positively correlated with EC and OM. Kuttanad region experienced the worst ever flooding in its history, upsetting many model farms and farming system in there.

Flood impacted paddy field of Kuttanad

CHAPTER - 5

MAJOR CONSTRAINS IN RICE PRODUCTION

Rice production in Kuttanad region has several constrains that could negatively impact on the sustainable rice problem

- **Monsoon Flood**

The topographical features of Kuttanad are unique. It is not possible to cultivate rice in Kuttanad region during monsoon season due to inland water flood, and this area will remain submerged for whole season. Since the area is water-logged, cultivation is carried out by enclosing small areas within dykes or bunds and pumping out the water. After April, due to high tide, saline water intrusion may occur (Jayan and Sathyanathan, 2010).

- **Salinity**

The soils are affected by severe acidity and periodic saline water inundation with consequent accumulation of soluble salts. This is a yield limiting factor (Devi et al., 2017). After April, due to high tide when sea water enters these areas causes saline water intrusion (Jayan and Sathyanathan, 2010).

- **Acidity**

Soil acidity causes nutrient stress to rice (Mandal *et al.,* 2003) and is a main barrier to rice production. The pH of Kuttanad soils is below 4.0 due to the formation of sulphuric acid by the oxidation of pyrites (Neenu *et al.,* 2020). Formation of acid components is the result of deep penetration of oxygen into iron pyrite layer. As the water table rapidly rises with the rainfall, Al, Fe and Mn are also brought to the topsoil, which increases the acidity and toxicity (Minh *et al.,* 1998). Abundance of Fe, Al and Mn causes P deficiency to plants (Pons and Kevie, 1969).

- **Fe, Al and Mn - Toxicity**

Kuttanad soils are rich in Fe, Mn and Al concentration. Continuous submergence of Kuttanad soils maintains the concentration of these toxic substances. The extractable and water soluble Al content of these soils also increased due to the persistence of a pH below 4.5 (Raju 1988; KAU 1994). Draining out of this toxicated water to the external canals may cause the termination of aquatic organisms (Nair and Pillai, 1990). Typical Fe toxicity symptoms are generally manifested as tiny brown spots starting from the tips and spreading towards the bases of the lower leaves and purple bronzing, yellow, or orange discoloration of the lower leaves may occur (Sahrawat, 2005).

- **Low Nutrient Content**

In the absence of iron and aluminum toxicity and harmful salinity, phosphorus and bases like Ca, Mg, K, Zn, Cu deficiency is the most important problem of acid sulfate soils (Attanandana and Vacharotayan, 1986). The presence of excess quantities of Al, Fe and H in soil had antagonistic effects on bases. The extent of deficiency may vary with parent material and other soil forming factors.

Table 5: Nutrient status of rice growing Kuttanad soils

Av. N	Av. P	Av. K	Av. Ca	Av. Mg	Av. Fe
	kg/ha			mg/kg	
333	13.81	515.20	318.58	23.58	423.13

Av. Cu	Av. Mn	Av. Zn	Av. B	Av. Si
		mg/kg		
0.49	6.00	2.79	0.08	11.27

In table 5, you can see the Nutrient status of kuttanad soils where nitrogen and phosphorous are in medium rate while K, Fe and Mn are in higher rate, and others are in low concentration

- **Akiochi Disease**

Kuttanad acid sulphate soils are typic Sulfaquept of low permeability. Several weeks of flooding may causes reducing of sulphate to sulphide and may also form FeS which results in the formation of Fe^{2+} in soil solution. Hence it leads to the formation of low concentrations of H_2S in soil solution (Yoshida, 1981; Van Breemen, 1993). H_2S can be toxic to rice at the very low concentration of 1 ppm (Mitsui, 1955). It manifests as akiochi disease. The symptoms like black root rot with stunted plants and leaf chlorosis are observed.

CHAPTER - 6

CONSTRAIN MANAGEMENT

➢ Neutralization of Acidity

To ameliorate soil acidity, practice of liming is adopted in Kuttanad soils. This can enhance the physical, chemical and biological properties of acid soils (Bolan, 2003). Thereby yield limiting factors like low pH and resultant problems such as Fe toxicity and low availability of other nutrients are resolved. Burnt lime shell (calcium oxide) is the most common liming material used in Kerala. But due to cheaper cost dolomite is also in usage (Devi *et al.,* 2017). KAU (2016) has recommended application of dolomite @450Kg ha^{-1} as two splits. In a comparative study on lime and dolomite Devi *et al.* (2017), pointed that lime could neutralize the pH effectively, meanwhile dolomite enhances the crop growth and yield. Also the application of ameliorants enhances the availability of P in soil.

Table 6: Neutralizing value of liming materials

Liming Materials	Neutralizing Value
Burnt lime	**179**
Slaked lime	**136**
Dolomite	**109**
Lime	**100**
Slag	**86**

Phosphogypsum	**0.33**

Table 6, shows the liming materials and their neutralizing value. It depicts that on applying, burnt lime is having higher neutralizing value of 179 followed by slaked lime and dolomite with 136 and 109 respectively. Neutralizing value explains the amount of acid, that a given weight of liming material will neutralize

Table 7: Effect of ameliorants and their time of application on soil pH

Treatments	30 DAS	Before PI Stage
Lime in two splits as basal and at 30 DAS; (T1)	6.13	5.4
Lime in two splits as basal and one week before third dose of fertilizer application (T2)	5.07	6.07
Dolomite in two splits as basal and at 30 DAS(T3)	5.47	5.13
Dolomite in two splits as basal and one week before third dose of fertilizer application (45 days) (T4)	5.07	5.53
Rice husk ash in two splits as basal and at 30 (T5)	5.03	5.03
Rice husk ash in two splits as basal and one week before third dose of fertilizer application (T6)	4.7	4.8
Control (T 7)	4.53	4.6
LSD(0.05)	0.258	3.502

The study of devi and co workers, potraying the effect of ameliorants on soil pH. •They have used 7 treatments including lime, dolomite, rice husk ash in two splits. From the table, At 30 DAS, where lime, dolomite and Rice Husk Ash used as basal and 30 DAS has recorded a higher soil pH compared to, lime dolomite and Rice Husk Ash applied as basal and before PI stage.

But Soil test at before PI stage showed better pH for soil, where lime, dolomite and Rice Husk Ash applied as basal and before PI stage compared to other treatments Which is exact opposite of soil test data at 30 DAS. •From the experiment, it is concluded that application of dolomite, lime or Rice Husk Ash can effectively reduce acidity in very strongly acidic soils of Kuttanad region. •Also they can improve soil available Ca and Mg.

Table 8: Effect of ameliorants and their time of application on yield attributes of rice

Treatments	Number of panicles	Sterility percentage	1000 grain weight	Grain yield (t ha^{-1})	Benefit-cost ratio
T_1	216.67	8.93	26	7.58[a]	2.69
T_2	223.33	9.60	24.33	6.46	2.3
T_3	290	8.40	25.33	7.92	2.84
T_4	200	9.27	26.33	7.02	2.52
T_5	256.67	8.00	25.67	7.59	2.72
T_6	210	8.67b	25.67	6.98	2.63
T_7	130	16.87	23	4.31	1.62
LSD(0.05)	**38.986**	**1.315**	**NS**	**0.851**	**0.308**

In the same study, another part is the effect of ameliorants on yield attributes. With the same treatments as discussed above. This table depicts that... the highest grain yield was obtained for dolomite application in two splits as basal and at 30 DAS which is treatment 3, but it was on par with Rice Husk Ash and lime applied at basal and 30 DAS. Which is T1 and T5. The sterility percentage was lower for dolomite and Rice Husk Ash applied as basal and 30 DAS and the highest for control. The 1000 grain weight was also higher for ameliorants. In addition BC Ratio is found higher from Dolomite application. These datas can covey that ameliorants can also influence plant growth

- **Biochar application**

Biochar is an organic amendment, with slightly alkaline pH (7.9), therefore in high concentration it can reduce soil acidity and also can be substitute for lime materials (Rodríguez *et al.*, 2009; Masulili, 2010). In a comparative study of Padmakumar and Thomas (2013), on the effect of biochar and other selected amendments on rice growth and soil properties, they concluded that biochar application would reduce leaching, increase N retention and P and K availability, enhance microbial biomass, improve water holding capacity, expand soil carbon pool and increase rice yield.

Table 9: Effect of biochar and other amendments on soil characteristics

Treatments	pH	Conductivity (ms)	CEC (C mol kg^{-1})	N (%)	P (kg/ha)	K (ppm)
Control	4.4±0.17	0.56±0.02	9.5±0.13	0.06±0.02	13.88±0.66	48.5±0.57
C_E	4.4±0.12	0.68±0.04	9.4±0.17	0.12±0.01	31.36±0.86	34±0.86
C_P	4.4±0.07	0.64±0.02	9.9±0.13	0.09±0.02	27.78±0.94	36.5±0.68
C_F	5.2±0.17	0.64±0.03	10.0±0.11	0.12±0.02	33.60±0.79	54.5±1.18
B_{15}	4.8±0.11	0.72±0.05	10.1±0.06	0.08±0.01	32.20±0.28	58±0.69
B_{25}	5.4±0.28	0.49±0.05	10.5±0.11	0.09±0.02	33.74±0.47	62±0.46
B_{35}	5.5±0.07	0.43±0.04	10.6±0.17	0.17±0.03	37.77±0.79	69±1.02

C_E Compost –*Eichhornia* – 25 gm

C_P Compost- *Pueraria – 25 gm*

C_F Chemical Fertilizer-

Superphosphate -5 gm

B_{15} Biochar - 15 gm

B_{25} Biochar - 25 gm

B_{35} Biochar - 35 gm

The table 9 from that study of Padmakumar and Thomas (2013), application of soil amendments produced significant variations in the physical and chemical properties of the soil. The highest pH value was observed in the trial treated with maximum biochar, while the lowest values were recorded in the control. It has higher CEC, so it has the ability to supply more ca, mg and potassium. In addition organic matter could supply significant amount of NPK than other amendments. But all these values for chemical fertilizers are in par with biochar, and composts showing distinctive variation from biochar.

- **Application of Organic matter**

According to Pocknee & Sumner (1997) application of organic matter provides an alkalizing effect in acid sulphate soils than addition of inorganic salts (e.g. Ca_2SO_4). It is well known that carbonic and other organic acids are produced by organic matter oxidation. Commonly used organic matter sources are plant residues that can improve soil fertility, recycle nutrients and maintain moisture content. OM is cheap and easily available for farmers. Organic compounds such as sodium malate, sodium citrate, calcium oxalate or calcium gluconate can raise soil pH (Yan *et al.*, 1996). Application organic multinutrient pellets containing blood meal and rock phosphate improved the N, P, K and micronutrient concentration of soil (Rohith *et al.,* 2023). It also contributed a liming effect in soil, where pH of the soil found increased.

- **Breeding of Varieties**

Acidity, salinity and sulphide injury limits the rice production in Kuttanad soils. So it is necessary to choose the crop wisely to deal with those problems. During 1998 RRS, Moncompu released 2 rice varieties tolerant to soil problems, named Karishma and Krihnanjana which can tolerate acidity and sulphide injury and can give moderate levels of yield to farmers. Later more varieties has released from this research institution such as Kallada champavu, Kochathikkira etc,. (Kumari, 2012).

- **Cropping system**

As rice is the supreme crop in acid sulphate soils of Kuttanad, the cropping pattern / system is also rice based. Common cropping system followed is Rice- Rice- Water fallow and Water fallow- Rice- Rice. Cropping system defines how effectively the land and nutrients in it is used (KAU, 2016).

- **Fe-Toxicity**

According to Thampatti *et al.* (2005) and Mini and Lekshmi (2021) lime application is the first practice to resolve the Fe-toxicity problems. Also Thampatti *et al.* (2016), mentioned about phytomining, an exploitation of phytoremediation potential of few promising aquatic macrophytes for the removal of Fe from acid sulphate wetland ecosystems.

On 2016, thampatti and coworkers done a study on Phytomining which is an effective plant-based technology suitable for the cleanup of aquatic ecosystems contaminated with toxic metals. This is done against the fe toxicity of kuttanad soils and they found that *Eichhornia crassipes* remove more iron from the ecosystem.

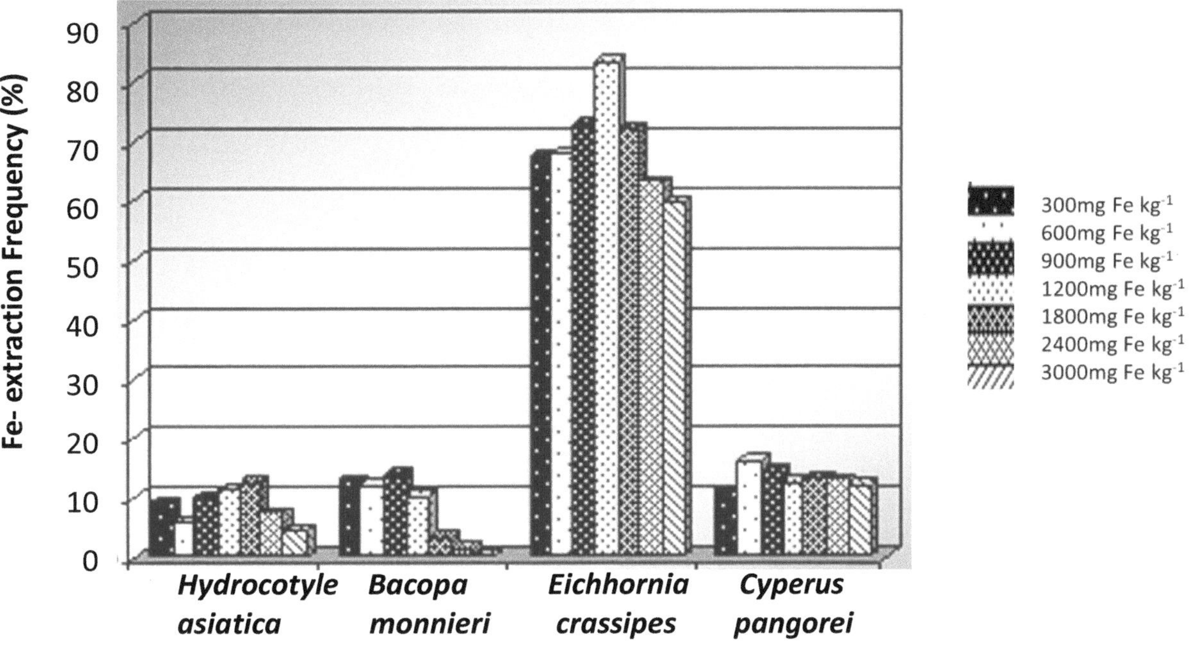

Figure 1: Fe toxicity management by aquatic macrophytes

This study is giving idea on Fe toxicity management by aquatic macrophytes. They have used *Hydrocotyle asiatica, Bacopa monnieri, Eichhornia crassipes, Cyperus pangorei* for their experiment. On assessing the removal of applied Fe, it was observed that *Eichhornia crassipes* alone showed very high extraction efficiency. Though the quantity of Fe removed increased with levels of Fe, the Fe extraction efficiency increased upto 1200mg fe/Kg and later it decreased. The general mechanisms behind Fe extraction by hyperaccumulators are either acidification of soil solution by excretion of protons or organic acids or chelation of Fe by plants. Hence fe toxicity is reduced.

Mini and Lekshmi (2021) established a new low cost environmental friendly organic treatment of rice husk ash, along with a customized nutrient formulation. It has shown 23% increase in the yield. In this study on Fe toxicity management using Rice Husk Ash (RHA) (table 10) we can depict that the treatment no.7 recorded the highest grain yield of 6.83 t ha-1 and straw yield of 8.57t ha^{-1} and was on par with Treatment 5 and Treatment 6. This indicates that application of rice husk ash as soil ameliorant is equally effective as lime in ameliorating the soil acidity and thereby increasing the grain and straw yield of rice.

Table 10: Fe toxicity management using Rice Husk Ash (RHA)

Treatments	Yield (t ha^{-1})	
	Grain	Straw
T1: Recommended dose of fertilizers (RDF) + lime	5.57	8.57
T2: Soil test based RDF (Stb RDF) and lime based on pH	5.86	8.44
T3: Stb RDF+RHA @ lime based on pH	5.93	8.37
T4: Stb RDF+ RHA @1/2 lime based on pH	5.4	8.3
T5: T1 + foliar spray of 0.5% solution of customized formulation at tillering and panicle initiation stage	6.43	8.5
T6: T2 + Foliar spray of 0.5% solution of customized formulation at tillering and panicle initiation stage	6.5	8.4
T7: T3 + Foliar spray of 0.5% solution of customized formulation at tillering and panicle initiation stage	6.83	8.57
T8: T4 + Foliar spray of 0.5% solution of customized formulation at tillering and panicle initiation stage	6.02	8.35
T9: 50% Stb RD + RHA@ lime in T2 + Foliar spray of 0.5% solution of customized formulation at tillering and panicle initiation stage	4.23	7.41
CD(0.05)	0.53	0.83

In addition, Thampatti *et al.* (2005) studied on the Fe toxicity management by integration of genetic tolerance and nutrition. Here integration genetic tolerant varieties (Phalguna) with proper nutrition may enhance rice yield.

For the study they have used 4 different treatments as no lime, ½ lime, full lime and recommended fertilizer treatments. 3 plant varieties have used for the study, such as Fe tolerant Phalguna, sensitive Prakash and locally preferred Jyothi Root characters and Fe toxicity scores were observed in this study. According to this table, the results indicates that varieties and levels of lime and fertilizers have significantly influenced grain and straw yield. Highest grain yield recorded by Phalguna which received ½ lime and 150% dose of P&K. These yields were significantly superior to those of locally preferred variety Jyothi. But ½ lime and 150% dose of N and K application increased yield in Jyothi. Influence of liming was significant at higher doses of NP&K fertilizers, indicating the need for a higher level of nutrients for rice in fe toxic acid sulphate soils. This also confirms the urgency to have genetically improved cultivars and identify locally preferred varieties.

Table 11: Grain yield and Fe content as influenced by lime and fertilizer and variety

	Grain yield (t ha^{-1}) and Fe content (mg kg^{-1})					
Treatment[a]	Phalguna		Prakash		Jyothi	
	I	II	I	II	I	II
No lime	3.10 (275)	3.22 (202)	2.73 (296)	2.82 (261)	2.97 (280)	2.99 (260)
½ LR	4.45 (272)	4.81 (161)	2.97 (288)	3.02 (245)	3.09 (234)	3.46 (211)
Full LR	3.62 (296)	3.82 (232)	2.77 (314)	2.85 (294)	3.02 (302)	3.15 (249)
Recommended practice	3.80 (279)	3.95 (250)	2.81 (316)	2.88 (298)	3.01 (308)	3.16 (278)
Mean (varieties)	3.85 (246)		2.86 (289)		3.11 (265)	
Fertilizers			I—3.20 (288) II—3.34 (245)			
CD (0.05)						
	Lime		0.076 (ns)[b]			
	Varieties		0.049 (29.9)			
	Fertilizer		0.040 (18.1)			

The highest yield is recorded by Phalguna with ½ lime application. Variety and fertilizer level had significantly influenced only the fe content of straw, which was much higher than that of grain. In both grain and straw fe content was lowest for phalguna and highest for prakash. Also among the levels of lime ½ lime recorded the lowest fe content. also application of P&K fertilizers had significantly reduced fe content in both grain and straw. Which indicates the favourable influence of liming anda higher fetilizer dose on fe toxicity in acid sulphate soils.

Table 12: Straw yield and Fe content as influenced by lime and fertilizer and variety

Treatment[a]	Straw yield (t ha^{-1}) and Fe content (mg kg^{-1})					
	Phalguna		Prakash		Jyothi	
	I	II	I	II	I	II
No lime	3.51 (388)	4.43 (370)	4.45 (428)	4.57 (423)	3.10 (422)	3.23 (404)
½ LR	4.96 (376)	5.28 (351)	4.66 (415)	4.96 (385)	3.28 (381)	3.81 (342)
Full LR	4.43 (396)	4.85 (372)	4.62 (406)	4.87 (398)	3.07 (396)	3.51 (378)
Recommended practice	4.49 (383)	4.93 (365)	4.28 (414)	4.52 (399)	3.14 (405)	3.53 (383)
Mean (varieties)	4.61 (365)		4.59 (409)		3.34 (389)	
Fertilizers			I—4.00 (401) II—4.38 (381)			
CD (0.05)			0.058 (13.8) 0.050 (11.9) 0.041 (9.8)			

- **Akiochi Disease**

Hydrogen sulphide has been shown to be toxic to the rice plant through its suppression of the oxidizing power of the roots. Prolonged submergence and soil reduction diminish the H_2S concentration. Establishing controlled and proper drainage system could reduce the H_2S effect (Attanandana and Vacharotayan, 1986).

- **Rice-Shrimp Cropping**

Shrimbs are grown in flooded soils of Kuttanad along with rice to make use of brackish water and to compensate the losses of rice due to flooding. This arrangement also reduces the production cost of rice since the soil is soft and clean (Jayan and Sathyanathan, 2010). This system keeps the sulphitic material flooded and thereby stops acid generation (Xuan, 1993).

- **Fertilizer Recommendations**

In Kuttanad soils K status is medium to high based on soil test data and also where incorporation of straw is in practice and tidal contribution of the nutrient is significant. While phosphorus can be skipped for six seasons without any significant reduction in grain yield in riverine alluvium soils medium to high in available P. In such condition, for rice KAU (2016) is recommending fertilizer dose of N, P_2O_5, K_2O as 90: 45: 15 respectively. Wherever wet broadcasting (direct seeding) is adopted, the first basal application of the nitrogen is given at the time of letting in water, after drying the field. Water-soluble phosphorus is applied as two split doses in Kuttanad region, as basal and at maximum tillering stage (KAU, 2016).

- **Water Management**

Drain out standing water from the main field and plough the field thoroughly. The petti and para is widely used to dewater the fields. Ensure a smooth and levelled field. Maintain a thin film of water to facilitate sowing so that the germinated seeds do not get covered with clayey soil. In Kari soils, avoid cracking of soils by prolonged drying since it will lead to severe acidity. Provide surface drains of 20 cm width and depth within the field at 10-20 m interval or running diagonally and join them with surface drain of 30 cm width and depth taken along the perimeter of the field (KAU, 2016).

Table 13. Management practices for the major constraints in acid sulphate soils. (adapted from Rohith, *et al*., (2024))

Major constraints	**Possible Management**
Monsoon flood	• Irrigation scheduling • Drainage management • Application of organic matter • Alteration in nutrient timing • Optimized plant density • Selection of suitable variety • Application of soil amendments • Establish buffer strips
Soil salinity	• pH management using gypsum (calcium sulfate) • Field margins • Periodic soil monitoring • pH neutralization • Regulate the use of potassic fertilizers • Reduced plant population • Manage the soil EC level
Soil acidity	• Lime application (calcium carbonate) • Sulfur management • Application of organic amendments • Avoid prolonged water logging • Buffer strip establishment • Resistant varieties • Regulate the fertilizer application • Controlled irrigation • Neutralize the soil pH
Fe, Al and Mn Toxicity	• Lime amendment

	• Use tolerant crops • Use cover crops • Incorporate antagonists to the soil • Application of organic matter • Use chelating agents • Use phytoremediation techniques
Low nutrient content	• Liming to increase pH • Organic matter management • Regulate the use of phosphoric fertilizer • Use ammoniacal fertilizers • Reduce the use sulphate fertilizers (or sulphur fertilizers) • Use slow release fertilizers • Application of organic soil amendments • Split application of fertilizers

CHAPTER - 6

CONCLUSION

Kuttanad, a low-lying region below mean sea level in Kerala, India, is renowned for its unique acid sulfate soils and extensive rice cultivation. The region's soils are highly diverse and form the foundation of its distinctive farming systems, which have adapted to the challenging environmental conditions. A key characteristic of these soils is their extreme acidity, with pH levels often below 4.5, primarily due to the presence of acid-forming components such as jarosites and pyrites. The proximity to the sea exacerbates the situation, leading to frequent seawater intrusion, which significantly increases soil salinity. Together, these factors create a challenging environment for rice cultivation, as they not only limit nutrient availability but also lead to toxicities caused by elevated levels of aluminum (Al), iron (Fe), manganese (Mn), soluble salts, and hydrogen sulfide (H_2S). These toxic elements pose significant physiological stress to rice plants, affecting their growth, yield, and nutrient uptake.

Over the years, several studies have explored the constraints to rice production in Kuttanad and have proposed various management strategies to address these challenges. Research has focused on identifying specific soil and water conditions that limit crop productivity and developing interventions to mitigate these issues. For example, strategies like liming to neutralize soil acidity, application of organic amendments, and the use of saline-resistant and acid-tolerant rice varieties have shown promise. These studies not only enhance our understanding of the intricate relationship between soil chemistry and crop performance in this unique agroecosystem but also contribute to the development of comprehensive management practices. Such insights are vital for improving rice productivity in Kuttanad while ensuring the sustainability of its fragile ecosystem, making the region a model for addressing similar challenges in other parts of the world.

DISCUSSION

1. **How to identify Iron toxicity in rice growing soils?**

   Leaves appear purple-brown if Fe toxicity is severe. Stunted growth, extremely limited tillering also may occur. Coarse, sparse, damaged root system with a dark brown to black coating on the root surface and many dead roots. Freshly uprooted rice hills often have poor root systems with many black root

2. **What are the symptoms of hydrogen sulphide toxicity?**

   Interveinal chlorosis of emerging leaves coarse, sparse, dark brown to black root system. Freshly uprooted rice hills often have poorly developed root systems with many black roots (stains of Fe sulfide) unlike healthy roots, which are covered with a uniform and smooth orange-brown coating of Fe3+ oxides and hydroxides.

3. **Management practices for H_2S toxicity in acid sulphate soils.**

   Prolonged submergence (which could keep the sulphitic material flooded and stops acid generation) and soil reduction (through leeching) diminishes the H_2S concentration. Establishing controlled and proper drainage system also reduces the H_2S effect.

4. **Major changes occurred in rice fields after flood in Kuttanad?**

   Soil pH slightly increased, but organic matter decomposition rate reduced, bulk density and particle density found to be reduced. Accumulation of more salts observed. Increase in water holding capacity of soil and more soil water movement. Accumulation of more silts were reported and on drying soil found to be cracked.

5. **Another place in India which is similar to characteristics of Kuttanad soil?**

   Sunderbans

   (West Bengal)

6. **What is the difference between labile carbon and active carbon?**

   Labile carbon is the fraction of soil organic carbon with most rapid turnover times and its oxidation drives the flux of CO_2 between soils and atmosphere. It is the most sensitive pool available relatively in small proportion as it is easily affected by fluctuation in environmental conditions. Active carbon is an indicator of the small portion of soil organic matter that can serve as a readily available food and energy source for the soil microbial community, thus helping to maintain a healthy soil food web.

7. **Does biochar have any influence on water retention?**

   Because of its porous nature, biochar can improve your soil's water retention and water holding capacity – defined as the amount of water that a soil can hold for its crops – so that your plants will have more water available to them for a longer period of time. Experimental studies show that application of biochar affects soil water retention, which could be attributed to high porosity, presence of hydrophilic domains and large specific surface area of biochar.

8. **Is it possible to follow any crop rotation practices in Kuttanad low land?**

   Soils of Kuttanad mostly saturated or submerged in condition. So it is not possible to other crops than rice. Crop rotation of rice itself only is possible. But as a rotation rice can be followed by fish or shrimp. This s followed in various parts of Kuttanad.

REFERENCES

Aparna, B., Gladis, R., Aryanath, V., and Thampatti, K.C.M. 2020. Studies on the Acid Sulphate Soils of Kuttanad of Kerala. *Ind. J. Pure App. Biosci.* 8(2): 421-428.

Arya Lekshmi, V. 2016. Silicon availability of tropical soils with respect to Rice nutrition, Ph.D thesis. College of Horticulture, Vellanikkara.

Arya, V. S. 2020. Assessment of soil quality in the post flood scenario of AEU 4 in Alappuzha district of kerala and generation of GIS Maps. MSc (Ag) College of Agriculture, Vellayani.

Attanandana, T. and Vacharotayan, S. 1986. Acid sulfate soils: Their characteristics, genesis, amelioration and utilization. *J. Southeast Asian Stud.* 24(2): 154-180.

Beena, V. I. 2005. Land evaluation and crop suitability rating of the acid sulphate soils of Kuttanad for sustainable land use planning. Ph .D. thesis. Kerala Agricultural University, Thrissur. 207p.

Bindu, J. and Ramabhadran, A. 2011. Study on cement stabilized Kuttanad clay. In *Proc., Indian Geotechnical Conf*: 465-68p.

Bloomfleld, C. and Coulter, J.K. 1974. Genesis and management of acid sulfate soils. *Adv. in Agron.* 25: 265-326.

Bolan, N. S., Adriano, D. C., and Curtin, D. 2003. Soil acidification and liming interactions. *Adv. in Agron.* 78: 215-72.

Chacko, F. M., Sreekanth, N. P., Shanthi, P.V., Padmakumar, B., and Thomas, A.P. 2014. Soil Carbon Dynamics and Global Warming Potential of Selected Soil Series and Landuse Categories. *Octa J. of Env. Res*: 2(1).

Chattopadhyay, S. and Sidhardhan, S. 1985. Regional analysis of the greater Kuttanad, Kerala. Technical Report No. 43. Centre for Earth Studies, Trivandrum, India.

Chenery, E.M., 1954. Acid sulphate soils in Central Africa. *Trans. 5th Int. Cong. Soil Sci. Leopoldville*. 4: 195-198.

Dalal, R.C. 1975. Urease activity in some Trinidad soils. *Soil Biology and Biochemistry*, 7(1):5-8.

Devi, V.S., Swadija, O.K., Geetha, K. and Mathew, R. 2017. Acidity amelioration for rice yield enhancement in acid sulphate (Vaikom kari) soils of Kuttanad in Kerala. *J. of Crop and Weed*, 13(3): 78-81.

Dhanya, K. R. 2017. Assessment of soil carbon pools in acid sulphate soils of Kuttanad. Master's thesis, Department of Soil Science and Agricultural Chemistry, College of Agriculture.

Fores, E. and Comin. F.A. 1987. Chemical characteristics of the water in the rice fields. *Soil Sci. Soc. Am.* J. 66: 544-553.

Gomez, A., 2016. The Soil Physical, Chemical and Biological Properties. *J. of Trop. Soils*. 15 – 27p.

Indira, B.V.N. and Covilakom, M.T.K. 2013. Characterization of acidity in acid sulphate soils of Kerala. *J. Life sci.* 7(8): 907.

Jayan, P. R. and Sathyanathan, N. 2010. Overview of farming practices in the water-logged areas of Kerala, India. *Int. J. of Agric Biol.* 3(4): 28-43.

Jinbo, Z., Changchun, S., and Wenyan, Y. 2006. Land use effects on the distribution of labile organic carbon fractions through soil profiles. *Soil. Sci. Soc. Am. J.* 70(2): 660 - 667.

Juhrian, J., Yusran, F.H., Wahdah, R., and Priatmadi, B.J. 2020. The effect of biochar, lime, and compost on the properties of acid sulphate soil. *J. of Wet. Env. M.* 8(2): 157- 173.

Kabeerathumma, S. 1969. Effects of liming on exchangeable cations and availability of nutrients in acid soils of Kuttanad. M.Sc. (Ag.) thesis, University of Kerala, Thiruvananthapuram.

Kabeerathumma, S. 1975. Chemistry of low productive acid sulphate soils and their amelioration for growing rice. Ph.D. thesis, Orissa University of Agriculture and Technology,.Bhubaneshwar.

KAU [Kerala Agricultural Universit]. 1994. *A Glimpse to Problem Soils of Kerala.* Kerala Agricultural University, Thrissur, India.

KAU [Kerala Agricultural University]. 2016. Package of Practices Recommendations: Crops (15th Ed.). Kerala Agricultural University, Thrissur.

Kikuchi, H., Watanabe, T., Jia, Z., Kimura, M., and Asakawa, S. 2007. Molecular analysis reveal stability of bacterial communities in bulk soil of a Japanese Paddy field: Estimation by denaturing gradient gel electrophoresis of ssRNA genes amplified from DNA accompanied with RNA. *Soil Sci. Plant Nutr*. 53: 448-458.

Kiss, S., Dragan-Bularda, M., and Radulescu, D. 1975. Biological significance of enzymes accumulated in soil. In *Advances in agronomy*. 27: 25-87.

Kumari, S.L., 2012. Status Paper on Rice in Kerala.

Mandal, A. B., Basu, A.K., Roy, B., Sheeja, T.E., and Roy, T. 2003 Genetic management for increased tolerance to aluminum and iron toxicities in rice- *A rev. Ind. J. Bio*. 3: 359-68.

Masulili, A. 2010. Rice husk biochar for rice based cropping system in acid soil, the characteristics of rice husk biochar and its influence on the properties of acid sulfate soils and rice growth in west Kalimantan, *Indones. J. Agric. Sci*. 2: 39-47.

Minh, L. Q., Tuong, T.P., Mensvoort, M. E. F., and Bouma, J. 1998. Soil and water table management effects on aluminum dynamics in an acid sulphate soil in Vietnam. *Agric. Ecosyst. Environ.t* 68: 255-262.

Mini, V. and Lekshmi, S. 2021. Rice Husk Ash as a Low Cost Soil Ameliorant for Abating Iron Toxicity in Lowland Rice. *Agric. Sci. Dig*, 41(1).

Mitsui, S. 1955. *Inorganic nutrition, fertilization, and soil amelioration for lowland rice* 79(3): 230p.

Money, N. S. 1961. Studies on soils of Kuttanad, Part II: Microbiological nitrogen transformations in acid peat soils of Kuttanad. *Agric. Res. J of Kerala.* 1:52-58.

Money, N. S. and Sukumaran, K. M. 1973. Chemical, Microbiological and Agronomic Aspects of the acid Saline Waterlogged Soil of Kerala. Technical Bull. No. I. Directorate of Extension Education, Kerala Agricultural University, Mannuthy, Thrissur.

Nair, J .Y. and Subramoney, N. 1969. Studies on H_2S injury to rice plants. *Agric. Res. J. Kerala.* 7: 21-24.

Nair, P.V.R. and Pillai, V.K. 1990. Changing ecology of Vembanad Lake. Rice in Wetland Ecosystem. Kerala Agricultural University, Vellanikkara, Trissur. 280-285p.

Neenu, S., Karthika, K.S., Anilkumar, K.S., and Nair, K.M. 2020. Kuttanad soils: the potential acid sulphate soils of Kerala. *Harit Dhara E Magazine* 3(2):19-23.

Padmakumar, B., and Thomas, A.P. 2013. A study of the fertility and carbon sequestration potential of rice soil with respect to the application of biochar and selected amendments. *Annals of Environmental Science*. 7.

Padmakumar, K.G. 2013. Kuttanad-Global Agricultural Heritage: Promoting Uniqueness. *In Proc. Kerala Environ. Cong*: 62-74p.

Pillai and Subrahmanyan. 1929. Some peculiar low lying soils of central Travencore. *J. Ind. Insti. Sci.* 13: 3-10.

Pocknee, S. & Sumner, M.E. 1997. Cation and nitrogen contents of organic matter determine its soil liming potential. *Soil. Sci. Soc. Am. J.* 61: 86–92.

Poelman, J.N.B. 1973. Acid sulphate soils. *Soil Survey Institute.* 197p.

Ponnamperuma, F.N. 1984. Effects of flooding on soils. *Flooding and plant growth, 10*: 45p.

Pons, L.J. and Kevie, V.D. 1969. Acid sulphate soils in Thailand. *Soil survey report, Report SSPR.* 81-1969p.

Pulford, I. D. and Tabatabai, M. A. 1988. Effect of waterlogging on enzyme activities in soils. *Soil Biol. Biochem.* 20(2): 215-219.

Raju, P.V. 1988. Effect of drying and wetting on the physical, physico-chemical and chemical properties of the submerged soils of Kuttanad Ph. D. Thesis, Kerala Agricultural University, Thrissur.

Reichardt, W., Mascarina, G., Padre, B., and Doll, J. 1997. Microbial communities of continuously cropped, irrigated rice fields. *Appl. Enviro. Microbiol*. 63(1): 233-238.

Rohith, A.K, Gladis, R., Joseph, B., Rani, B. and Jose, N. 2023. Nutrient Release Characteristic of Multinutrient Pellet for Organic Farming in Rice (*Oryza sativa* L) for Acid Sulphate Soils. *Int. J Plant. Soil Sci.* 35(6): 1-18.

Rohith, A.K, Joseph, B., and Gladis, R. 2024. Probing Acid Sulphate Soils for Sustainable Rice Production in Kuttanad: Challenges and Solutions. *Ann. Res. Rev. Biol.* 39(12): 46-56

Rodríguez, L., Salazar, P., and Preston, T. R. 2009. Effect of biochar and bio digester effluent on growth of maize in acid soils. *Livest. Res. Rural Dev.* 21:110p

Sahrawat, K.Á. 2005. Iron toxicity in wetland rice and the role of other nutrients. *J. Plant Nutr*. 27(8): 1471-1504.

Schoner, A., Noubactep, C., Buchel, G., and Sauter, M. 2009. Geochemistry of natural wetlands in former uranium milling sites (eastern Germany) and implications for uranium retention. *Chemie der Erde-Geochem*., 69: 91-107.

Smily, J. M., Jacob, V., and Ravi Kumar, V. 2012. Soil microflora of paddy fields among different rice farming systems. *J. Acad. Ind. Res*. 1(1): 50p.

Suganya, K. and Sivapullaiah, P.V. 2015. Effect of changing water content on the properties of Kuttanad soil. *Geotech. Geol.l Eng.* 33(4): 913-921.

Thampatti, K. C. M. 1997. Morphological, physical and chemical characterization of the soils of North Kuttanad. Ph. D. Thesis, Kerala Agricultural University, Thrissur.

Thampatti, K. C. M., Cheri an, S., and Iyer, M.S. 2005. Managing iron toxicity in acid sulphate soils by integrating genetic tolerance and nutrition. *Int. Rice Res. Notes.* 30:37-39.

Thampatti, K.M., Beena, V. I., and Usha, P.B. 2016. Aquatic macrophytes for phytomining of iron from rice based acid sulphate wetland ecosystems of Kuttanad. *J Indian Soc Coast Agric Res. 34*(2): 1-6.

Thampatti, K.M. and Jose, A.I. 2000. Characterization of acid saline rice based wetland ecosystems of Kuttanad, Kerala, and their salinity protection by Thanneermukkom regulator. *Agropedology*, 10: 111-115.

Thornton, I. and Giglioli, M. E. C. 1965. The mangrove swamps of Keneba, Lower Gambia River Basin. II. Sulphur and pH in the profiles of swamp soils. *J. Appl. Ecol.* 257-269p.

Van Mensvoort, M. E. F., Van Ni, D. and Van der Schans, J. 1991. Improvement of acid sulphate soils by leaching with salt or brackish water. *Rice production on acid soils of the tropics*. 91: 219-224.

Van Breemen, N. 1973. Dissolved aluminum in acid sulfate soils and in acid mine waters. *Soil Soil. Sci. Soc. Am. J.* 37(5): 694-697.

Van Breemen, N. 1993. Environmental aspects of acid sulphate soils. In *Selected Papers Ho Chi Minh City Symp.* 391-402p.

Xuan, Vo Tong. 1993. Recent advances in irrigated land uses on acid sulphate soils. *Ho Chi Minh City Symp. on Acid Sulphate Soils*. 53: 129- 135.

Yang, Y., Guo, J., Chen, G., Yin, Y., Gao, R., and Lin, C. 2009. Effects of forest conversion on soil labile organic carbon fractions and aggregate stability in subtropical China. *Plant. Soil.* 323: 153-162.

Yan, F., Schubert, S., and Mengel, K. 1996. Soil pH changes during legume growth and application of plant materials. *Biol. Fert. Soils*. 23: 236–242.

Yoshida, S. 1981. Fundamentals of Rice Crop Science. *Int. Rice Res. Inst*. 471: 494p.

About the authors

Rohith A K

Ph. D. Scholar
Department of Soil Science and Agricultural Chemistry
College of Agriculture, Vellayani, Thiruvananthapuram
Kerala Agricultural University
rohith-2020-11-030@student.kau.in

Dr. Biju Joseph

Associate Professor
Soil Science and Agricultural Chemistry
Rice Research Station, Moncompu, Alappuzha
Kerala Agricultural University
biju.joseph@kau.in

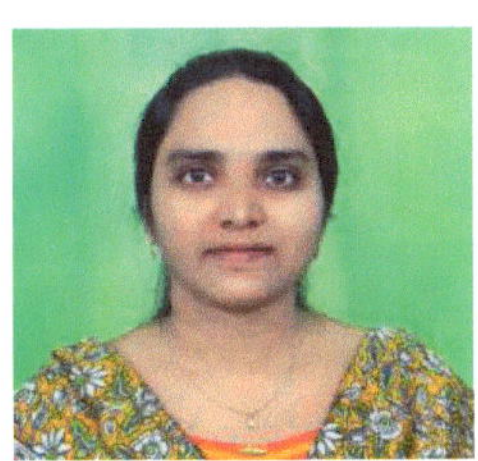

Dr. Kota Adilakshmi

Ph.D. (Agri)
Department of Soil Science and Agricultural Chemistry
College of Agriculture, Vellayani, Thiruvananthapuram
Kerala Agricultural University
adilakshmikota91@gmail.com

Rahul Chandra

Graduate Teaching Assistant
MS in Environmental and Soil Sciences
University of Tennessee, Knoxville
rchandr7@vols.utk.edu

Namitha Krishna

Ph. D. Scholar
Department of Agronomy
College of Agriculture, Vellayani, Thiruvananthapuram
Kerala Agricultural University
krishnanamitha09@gmail.com

www.ingramcontent.com/pod-product-compliance
Lightning Source LLC
LaVergne TN
LVHW071124160826
845679LV00005B/1169
* 9 7 9 8 8 9 6 9 9 6 3 2 3 *